THE LIVING

Anthony Clarvoe

BROADWAY PLAY PUBLISHING INC
New York
www.broadwayplaypublishing.com
info@broadwayplaypublishing.com

This play was first published in January 1996 in the collection *Plays By Anthony Clarvoe*.

First printing, this edition: August 2020
I S B N: 978-0-88145-875-6

Book design: Marie Donovan
Page make-up: Adobe Indesign
Typeface: Palatino

THE LIVING was presented as a workshop in the Mark Taper Forum's 1991 New Works Festival, directed by Oskar Eustis; in the Denver Center's U S West TheatreFest `92, directed by Nagle Jackson; in Carnegie Mellon's 1992 Showcase of New Plays, directed by Brian Kulik; and at Kenyon College, directed by Harlene Marley; and in readings at the Oregon Shakepeare Festival, the Playwrights' Center, and Upstart Stage.

The world premiere of THE LIVING was presented on 3 May 1993 by the Denver Center Theater Company, Donovan Marley, Artistic Director, in U S West TheatreFest `93. The cast and creative contributors were:

MR JOHN GRAUNT..Jamie Horton
MRS SARAH CHANDLER.......................Katherine Heasley
DR EDWARD HARMAN...............................Sean Hennigan
MRS ELIZABETH FINCH ....Kay Doubleday
SIR JOHN LAWRENCE...................... William M Whitehead
LORD BROUNKER ....Michael Santo
REV DR THOMAS VINCENT.......................... Richard Risso
Ensemble .... Douglas Harmsen, James Baker,
Michael Hartman

Director ....Nagle Jackson
Set .... Vicki Smith
Lighting...Charles R MacLeod
Costumes...Lyndall L Otto
Sound ....Joel Underwood
Stage manager .... Christopher C Ewing

ACKNOWLEDGMENTS

The events that took place in London in 1665 have survived thanks to the extraordinary testimony left by Captain John Graunt, Nathaniel Hodges, MD, Sir John Lawrence, the Reverend Dr Simon Patrick, Mr Samuel Pepys, and the Reverend Dr Thomas Vincent; and to a remarkable act of historical imagination, Daniel Defoe's novel *A Journal Of The Plague Year*. This script owes a handful of sentences, and its existence, to them.

Dozens of directors, actors, designers, dramaturgs, crew, and staff worked with uncommon dedication to bring THE LIVING into being. My particular thanks to Nagle Jackson, Oskar Eustis, Brian Kulick, Harlene Marley, and Tom Szentgyorgyi.

My thanks also to the Fund for New American Plays and the W Alton Jones Foundation for their generous financial support for THE LIVING.

CHARACTERS

MR JOHN GRAUNT, *early thirties, a scientist*
MRS SARAH CHANDLER, *late twenties, a shopkeeper's wife*
DR EDWARD HARMAN, *mid-thirties, a physician*
MRS ELIZABETH FINCH, *early forties, a searcher of the dead*
SIR JOHN LAWRENCE, *late forties, Lord Mayor, a merchant*
LORD BROUNKER, *early fifties, a cavalier*
REV DR THOMAS VINCENT, *thirties, a nonconformist minister*

Three men, twenties to forties, may play the following roles:

MAN 1:
MR SAWYER, *a cabinetmaker*
PAUL, SARAH's *brother, a shopkeeper*
LAWRENCE'S CLERK
FIRST CONSTABLE
ROBERT, *a smith from Walthamstow*

MAN 2:
MR MILLS, *an Anglican minister*
SECOND CONSTABLE
BROUNKER'S CLERK
ANDREW, *a shopkeeper from Walthamstow*

MAN 3:
DR GODDARD, *a physician*
JAMEY, a watchman
BILL, *a farmer from Walthamstow*

SETTING

Scene: London, 1665

Set: A lower level and a slightly raised upper level connected by steps. A few pieces of furniture come and go, but the stage is as bare as possible.

A NOTE ON STAGING

Throughout the action, until the very end, no one approaches within arm's reach of anyone else. The exception is HARMAN, *and only when he wears protective clothing. No object is handed directly from one person to another. Everyone on stage is isolated in space.*

For if they fall, the one will lift up his fellow:
but woe to him that is alone when he falleth;
for he hath not another to help him up.
Ecclesiastes 4:10

ACT ONE

Scene One

(On the steps: SARAH sits on one side, head on her arms. GRAUNT stands on the other side, holding a large sheet of paper, densely printed. He looks up.)

GRAUNT: Ague and Fever, 5,257. Chrisomes and Infants, 1,258. Consumption and Tissick, 4,808.

(GRAUNT turns upstage to look at:)

(On the upper level: DOCTOR HARMAN, wearing a protective suit which completely hides his features. He hovers around a cot with a still figure in it. The suit includes a bulbous headpiece that covers him to the neck. A long breathing tube, shaped much like a bird's beak, protrudes from the front. He wears long, heavy gloves and a floor-length cloak. The whole suit is black and he looks, in sum, like a giant crow wearing a tricorn hat.)

(GRAUNT turns back.)

GRAUNT: This is a publication that comes out every week. Has for sixty years now. Each parish reports: how many christened, how many died, what they died of. It's called the Bills of Mortality. People subscribe, glance through. At year's end, they publish a summary. Convulsion, 2,036. Dropsy and Timpany, 1,478.

(HARMAN *pulls a sheet over the body and crosses down the steps near, but not too near,* SARAH. *He pulls off his bird head.* HARMAN *speaks to* SARAH, *who nods.*)

GRAUNT: Frighted, 23. Grief, 46. Overlaid and Starved, 45. Plague, 110,596.

(HARMAN *exits.*)

GRAUNT: We did not know where it came from. We did not know what caused it. We had no way to stop it. For all we knew, it would never end. For all we knew, the world would end, in 1665. Bear that in mind. Judge what we did. For in this account it does not matter what becomes of me, or any of us. All that matters is what becomes of you. And what we did may be of use to you, if this ever should happen again. (*He exits.*)

FINCH: (*Off*) Sarah? Sarah?

(MRS FINCH *enters. She carries a white wand, the badge of office of a searcher of the dead.*)

FINCH: There you are. No, stay where you are, dear.

SARAH: I should get you something.

FINCH: No.

SARAH: Mrs Finch, come in and may I offer you something? I'll call the boy to go around, I don't know what there is in the house.

FINCH: Is everyone gone, then? No, don't you move. I'll just see him and be gone.

SARAH: He's all right. Everyone says he's all right.

FINCH: Where are the children?

SARAH: My sister has them.

FINCH: How are they?

SARAH: They're all right. Everyone's all right here. Truly.

FINCH: I should see him. Then we'd know.

SARAH: No, really, you don't have to.

FINCH: I do, though, you know. Won't take a moment.

SARAH: Can't you just leave him alone?

FINCH: Sarah, the parish needs to know what he had. What are the parish clerks going to do all day if they can't be writing down all the babies born and who their parents are and the dead and what their sickness was?

SARAH: The doctor said it was spotted fever.

FINCH: Did he?

SARAH: Yes. He did. So I don't see why you have to --

FINCH: Rumor.

SARAH: I don't underst—what rumor?

FINCH: You hear two houses have been shut up in Chancery Lane?

SARAH: I didn't know—I've been at his bedside here—

FINCH: Whole household locked in. A rumor got around they had the plague. (*Pause*) Believe me, you're lucky it's me that's here. When my husband died they sent an old drunk woman, some old drunkard I barely knew barged into my home to tell me what killed my man was the apoplexy. And it wasn't apoplexy, it was heart, as everyone said, as the doctor said, but she saw a red face and said apoplexy, and there he is in the register, now to the Day of Judgment, dead of apoplexy. Till he rise again and straighten it out.

SARAH: Everyone said spotted fever, Mrs Finch, ask anyone.

FINCH: Not everyone, Sarah. What they say is one thing, but where have they gone?

SARAH: He's gone. There's nothing more to do here.

FINCH: Nothing? And no one to gather around you, grieving alone?

SARAH: They left because he's gone. That's all. He's gone.

FINCH: And they didn't want to go with him. But your children are all right?

SARAH: They've been with my sister.

FINCH: I should drop around there.

SARAH: I didn't let them touch him. I didn't let the children touch him, I didn't let his sister touch him or his mother touch him or anyone, no one touched him at all.

FINCH: Lonely death. No one there.

SARAH: I was there.

FINCH: Touching him.

SARAH: Sometimes.

FINCH: And now you'll want to see your children. And touch them, too. So you see? It's important what people know.

SARAH: Would we have to be quarantined?

FINCH: Only if it's the plague.

SARAH: It's not.

FINCH: That's what I'm here to decide. (*Pause*) Now, if you like, when I visit the children—for which the parish gives me not a thing, this is my concern as a neighbor now—if there's something you'd like me...to take for them?

SARAH: A message?

FINCH: A message, yes, but even if you had something you wanted me to take. For them. For their comfort? To make sure they *stay* comfortable? (*Pause*) Isn't that what we all want, Sarah, that the children be comfortable and safe?

SARAH: Mrs Finch. There is something? If you could?

FINCH: Is there?

SARAH: If you could...keep it for me?

FINCH: If that's what you'd like.

SARAH: We've been saving it. To keep the wolf from the door. But now— it's not a lot.

FINCH: That's fine. I know you, Sarah, you're a good girl. (*She crosses up the steps past* SARAH.) And now I'll have a quick look—

SARAH: Spotted fever, it's—he ran a fever, and—red spots, and— everyone said—*everyone* said. Before they went away.

(FINCH *peers at the figure in the cot and crosses quickly back down the steps.*)

FINCH: What do you know. Spotted fever.

SARAH: Is—is it?

FINCH: Now you know.

SARAH: Is it really? The children—

FINCH: Now if you'll tell me where you've got that little something—

SARAH: Let me get it for you—

FINCH: No! Stay where you are.

(*The lights fade on* SARAH *and* FINCH *as:*)

Scene Two

(Clamorous voices just offstage)

VOICES: *(Off)* I'm the next one in!
I don't care if he's in there!
I'll wait!

(On the lower level: Lights up as four men enter, at a cautious distance from each other. The first three have handkerchiefs over their faces and are wearing heavy cloaks. The last is GRAUNT *who, as he crosses, comes too close to* MAN 2.*)*

MAN 2: Watch yourself!

GRAUNT: Sorry.

MAN 1: *(Furthest into the room)* Give a man some breathing room, could you?

MAN 2: *(In the middle of the room)* All you want.

*(*MAN 2 *moves further from* MAN 1.*)*

MAN 3: Watch it!

MAN 2: Look, I've got him on the other side as well.

MAN 3: There's other rooms you could wait in.

MAN 2: Not if you want a pass. I came here for a pass.

MAN 1: You can wait the same as anyone.

*(*LAWRENCE *enters.)*

ALL: Sir! Sir John!

LAWRENCE: All right. Who is next?

ALL: Here!

LAWRENCE: Does everyone have a certificate of health from the College of Physicians?

MEN 2 & 3: Yes! Here!

MAN 2: Cost me enough.

MAN 1: Wait! They told me I had to go here first!

LAWRENCE: You're mistaken.

MAN 3: Got you good, son.

MAN 1: That's what they told me!

GRAUNT: Sir?

LAWRENCE: Anyone who wants a pass to leave London must go to the College for examination and return with a certificate of health.

MAN 1: Listen!

MAN 2: Clear out, would you?

LAWRENCE: I must have a certificate—

MAN 3: Here! Got mine here!

GRAUNT: Sir?

LAWRENCE: You, step forward.

MAN 2: Hey!

MAN 3: Thank you! Certificate, right here!

(MAN 3 *crosses toward* LAWRENCE *and places his certificate on the desk. He backs away and* LAWRENCE *looks at it without touching it, signs a piece of paper, places it next to the certificate, and backs away while* MAN 3 *crosses to the desk and takes the certificate and the pass, all during the following:)*

MAN 1: Friend? That certificate?

MAN 2: What of it?

MAN 1: How much for it?

MAN 2: Sorry, friend, I'm through dealing in them, I've saved this for myself.

LAWRENCE: Next!

MAN 1: Please.

MAN 2: Try outside. Certificate here!

LAWRENCE: You! How many are in the outer room?

MAN 3: Dozens.

GRAUNT: Fifty-three, actually.

LAWRENCE: Tell them to obey the constables and they'll all get a turn!

(MAN 2 *and* LAWRENCE *go through the same routine.*)

MAN 3: Hail and farewell, all!

MAN 1: Friend?

MAN 2: Thank you, Sir John!

(MAN 2 *exits.*)

MAN 1: That pass. You want to be careful who hears you have it. Thieves around.

MAN 3: Oh. Thanks. Well, I'm—

GRAUNT: Sir?

VOICES: (*Off*) Make way!

BROUNKER: (*Off*) Clear away there!

MAN 1: Why don't we go along together? Safety in numbers.

MAN 3: But you haven't got a pass yet.

MAN 1: Oh, I'll get one somehow. Coming?

VOICE: (*Off*) Clear a path for Lord Brounker!

(LORD BROUNKER *enters. Everyone bows.*)

BROUNKER: Hey ho, Jack.

LAWRENCE: Good morning, my Lord.

(MEN 1 *and* 3 *exit.*)

BROUNKER: No formalities, Jack, honestly, times like these.

LAWRENCE: It's good to see you, Harry. I'd started to think I was the only one left.

BROUNKER: I'm here on the King's business. Got your family out?

LAWRENCE: All out, settled in the country place.

BROUNKER: What about yourself? When do you go?

LAWRENCE: I'll be staying here.

BROUNKER: Jesus! Can't you leave it to the aldermen or something?

LAWRENCE: Harry. I'm an alderman.

BROUNKER: You're the Lord Mayor! Why can't you run things from a distance? Privy Council is.

LAWRENCE: Are they running things, or are they just running?

BROUNKER: Ho, Jack, gently now. All the best people are leaving.

LAWRENCE: What does that make you and me and the aldermen?

BROUNKER: The aldermen are excellent fellows, Jack, but surely you're a cut above them. We think of you as one of us. His Majesty himself, just before he left for Salisbury, said, "No one I'd rather have on the job than bully Jack Lawrence." He wants to know everything you do. I'm to be his eyes and ears.

LAWRENCE: Splendid, Harry! Who else is staying?

BROUNKER: Well, Albemarle is staying. But, Jack—

LAWRENCE: The Duke of Albemarle is upriver in Westminster.

BROUNKER: You don't want to work with him anyway. His physician told him the best preventive for the plague is a gallon of whiskey a day. He'll be drunk for the duration.

LAWRENCE: Aren't any of the Privy Council going to stay?

BROUNKER: Why do you need that pack of political lapdogs underfoot?

LAWRENCE: We'll need every figure of authority we can get. Together we may do this.

BROUNKER: Do what, exactly?

LAWRENCE: Harry. If all the best people are leaving, then all the worst people must be staying. They could riot in the streets any day. They might decide to loot your house.

BROUNKER: Ah. Can't the sheriffs keep them down?

LAWRENCE: They'll be no match for a mob.

BROUNKER: Call in the army.

LAWRENCE: It's a funny thing about armies. If you stand back and ask them to march into a plague they tend to resent you. They tend to become a mob. And so you have two mobs, and one of them has weapons.

BROUNKER: Ah.

LAWRENCE: The first thing we do is tell the Privy Council that we need enough money to keep the live people fed, the dying people indoors, and the dead people buried.

VOICES: (*Off*) Please! Sir! Can you give me a certificate, Sir!

GODDARD: (*Off*) I have business with the Lord Mayor!

VOICES: (*Off*) So do I!

GODDARD: (*Off*) I am with the College of Physicians!

LAWRENCE: Let him in!

(GODDARD *and* SAWYER *enter.* GODDARD *is wearing a protective suit like* HARMAN's. SAWYER *carries a roll of paper and measuring tools.* GODDARD *pulls off his headpiece.*)

GODDARD: Madness, madness.

LAWRENCE: Doctor Goddard. Good of you to come.

GODDARD: Good day, Sir John, the College has met and I have brought the proposed design.

BROUNKER: Goddard! Splendid, just the man—

GODDARD: Lord Brounker! What a surprise!

BROUNKER: Now I need your advice—

GODDARD: But, my Lord, I thought—

BROUNKER: This is about another matter.

(LAWRENCE *has noticed that* SAWYER *is sighting down his thumb at him.*)

LAWRENCE: Young man? May I help you?

GODDARD: Mr Sawyer will be taking your dimensions.

LAWRENCE: Goddard, why does the College of Physicians think that standing inside a box is going to keep me healthy?

BROUNKER: Hey what?

LAWRENCE: They want to display me in a glass cabinet, like a waxwork.

GODDARD: The wood and glass will interpose themselves between you and the contagious air your petitioners breathe at you. It is the same principle as the headpieces we doctors are wearing.

BROUNKER: Doesn't that scare the hell out of your patients?

GODDARD: The beak filters the infected air.

BROUNKER: And makes you look rather like a vulture.

GODDARD: Sir John, would you care to see the rendering of the box?

LAWRENCE: Please.

(SAWYER *unrolls the drawing and holds it up.*)

LAWRENCE: Jesus. I look like a prisoner in the dock.

GODDARD: If you want any modifications...

LAWRENCE: Give me some room to maneuver in there. A place to sit.

GODDARD: Note all this, would you, Sawyer?

LAWRENCE: A slot to pass papers in and out. A chamber pot. It'll save a little time.

BROUNKER: Goddard? If no air comes in—

GODDARD: Exactly, my Lord. The contagion—

BROUNKER: And no air goes out....

(*Pause*)

GODDARD: Air holes.

SAWYER: Hm.

GODDARD: Thank you, my Lord. Sawyer, sketch out a new design.

BROUNKER: Now listen, Goddard. Tell me what to do. I ordered a new suit a few weeks ago, beautiful silk, apple-blossom shade—you'd appreciate it, Jack, wasn't haberdashery how you made your pile?—friend in the haberdashers guild put me onto the silk, Thomason—

LAWRENCE: Ah yes—

BROUNKER: —took me down to the docks, pulled it right out of the crates for me, silk the color of apple blossom, floating in the breeze off the Thames. All the fittings, I'd slip it on and swear I could feel that breeze. Marvelous stuff. I sent the silk to my tailor—

LAWRENCE: Who does your— ?

BROUNKER: Meredith, well, and there's the difficulty. I took delivery today, and I've just heard he's fallen ill.

GODDARD: Plague?

BROUNKER: Maybe, maybe not, "fallen ill," that's all you hear anymore.

LAWRENCE: That's a shame. He does beautiful work. When do we see you wear the suit?

BROUNKER: Wear it? I'm afraid to have the damn thing in the house. Am I being stupid here?

GODDARD: My Lord is right to be cautious.

BROUNKER: I've told my man not to hang it in the wardrobe for fear of infecting the rest of my clothes.

GODDARD: Have your man fumigate it overnight in a fire made of sea coal.

BROUNKER: I can't visit his majesty smelling like a campfire.

GODDARD: It would be best not to wear the suit till the plague is past. By then the contagion should have faded.

BROUNKER: By then the fashion will have changed. (*He looks at the clothes he's wearing.*) He did do good work, didn't he. What a fucking waste.

VOICES: (*Off*) Hey! Wait your turn!

MILLS: (*Off*) I am a Doctor of Divinity!

LAWRENCE: Let him in!

BROUNKER: Is it always like this?

(*MILLS enters.*)

LAWRENCE: On the slow days.

MILLS: Sweet Jesus.

LAWRENCE: Good morning, Reverend Mills.

MILLS: Sir John, I have been inspecting the parishes as you asked?

BROUNKER: Hm?

LAWRENCE: We warn them that public gatherings are unhealthy, and they insist on praying together.

BROUNKER: Commendable, really. Stupid, but commendable.

LAWRENCE: Is there any means to keep the people away?

MILLS: From church? But, Sir John—

BROUNKER: Make the sermons more boring.

GODDARD: Impossible.

BROUNKER: True.

MILLS: I found most of the churches have no ministers. They seem to be leaving the city.

LAWRENCE: I don't believe it.

MILLS: Almost none of us are left.

BROUNKER: I thought London was lousy with preachers. Didn't we appoint cartloads of you people when we gave the fucking Puritans the toss?

LAWRENCE: First the court goes, now the clergy. Jesus, this town feels empty now all the cowards are leaving.

(Pause)

BROUNKER: The King has left London. Sir.

(Pause)

LAWRENCE: The King is the body of England. He has a duty to preserve himself.

BROUNKER: The man has a stallion's courage—

GODDARD: Stayed in town for weeks after the first case broke out—

BROUNKER: And a fucking magnificent king he is, gentlemen—

MILLS: Amen—

BROUNKER: Like a horse, God's my witness. Lady Castlemayne is swelling by the day, the ladies-in-waiting are pleading exhaustion—just to keep him from catching the pox, his physician has invented the cleverest little device.

GODDARD: I've heard. Ingenious man, Doctor Condom.

MILLS: Actually, I had intended to stay.

BROUNKER: Had you.

LAWRENCE: I am very pleased to hear it.

BROUNKER: Yes. How soldierly of you.

MILLS: And I pray many times a day that God maintain my resolve. Look at this.

(MILLS *pulls out a flier and places it on* LAWRENCE's *desk.)*

LAWRENCE: "Vacant churches for rent. Best offer accepted."

MILLS: My Lord, there has been an outbreak of satire.

LAWRENCE: Who is responsible?

MILLS: Dissenters and nonconformists. They are starting to return.

BROUNKER: Strictly illegal. Put them down, Jack. We're still running the prison ships. We'll crate them all up and dump them in America.

LAWRENCE: We'll arrest the leaders to start with. I'll try and talk sense to them. Thank you, Reverend Mills. Good day.

MILLS: Good day, Sir John. Good day, my Lord.

LAWRENCE: Mills. I thank God you are staying.

MILLS: Yes. May he grant me the strength.

LAWRENCE: Yes.

MILLS: As long as I possibly can. (*He exits.)*

LAWRENCE: I give him a week.

BROUNKER: You might as well give him a pass out of town right now.

GODDARD: Rightly so. I am sending all my patients to Salisbury with his majesty.

LAWRENCE: But, Goddard—

GODDARD: The air in the country is wholesome and fresh. A sovereign shield against distemper. The necessities of life in such times as these are more plentiful there, and there are just— fewer troubles in general. If we disperse, the plague passes over an empty place and the people can return when the weather turns healthy again.

LAWRENCE: Goddard. We have great need of physicians now.

GODDARD: Oh, I will do anything in my power for my patients. Do anything and go anywhere.

LAWRENCE: Splendid.

GODDARD: I would follow them to the ends of the earth, if necessary. And as my patients are almost exclusively attached to the court, I find I really have to go to Salisbury.

LAWRENCE: What about the people who are staying behind?

GODDARD: Who would that be?

LAWRENCE: Servants minding their masters' property. Laborers whose employers have shut their doors. Anyone who works for a living, and whose only work is here. The poor. Harry and I have to keep them from panicking. What will they do when they hear that the doctors have run?

GODDARD: Every physician I know has signed his own certificate of health and is packing to leave. What do you want us to do?

LAWRENCE: I want you to think of something. While you wait for your pass to be signed.

(Pause)

BROUNKER: Jack, you old horse trader.

GODDARD: Very well, Sir. The College of Physicians shall provide, free of charge, a list of preventives for the plague. We shall engage our chief apothecary to remain here and dispense medicines.

LAWRENCE: At the College's expense.

GODDARD: Agreed.

LAWRENCE: I need doctors. Talk to the College. I'll pay them at the public charge if I have to.

BROUNKER: Just a moment. Are you proposing that the government pay for medical care?

LAWRENCE: Harry, if we could talk about the means of payment later—

GODDARD: If money is forthcoming, we should find a few volunteers.

LAWRENCE: We'll find your money.

GODDARD: That would have to include pensions for their survivors.

LAWRENCE: Done.

GODDARD: Done. Good day then. My Lord, may I call on you in Salisbury? Your man came by for your certificate of health, I trust you received it?

LAWRENCE: Harry?

BROUNKER: Thank you, yes, I believe I have.

GODDARD: Good day, my Lord.

(As GODDARD *exits, the hubbub outside rises.*)

LAWRENCE: Harry...oh, Christ Almighty! (*He crosses to the door.*) All of you! Out! Come back in an hour!

(LAWRENCE *turns to* BROUNKER *as the hubbub subsides.*)

BROUNKER: The King wants me with him.

LAWRENCE: I thought you were here on his business.

BROUNKER: Not to stay.

LAWRENCE: Why can't you stay here? Travel down there.

BROUNKER: If I stayed here, they'd never receive me down there, would they.

LAWRENCE: I thought you were his majesty's eyes and ears.

BROUNKER: I am. And he doesn't want his eyes and ears to become diseased. When I come for your reports we're to meet on the outskirts of town. You'll be the hero, you know. Do your duty, and it's glory and everything. My duty, it seems, is to anticipate the King's desires and keep him amused.

LAWRENCE: Much in the manner of Lady Castlemayne.

(*Pause*)

BROUNKER: In the manner of a cavalier. And a friend of the King.

LAWRENCE: Why would he risk such a friend on a job like this?

BROUNKER: Well, because I insisted, didn't I. Had to do something.

LAWRENCE: Damn it, Harry, you're a good man, I need you here.

BROUNKER: To do what? What do you think you'll be doing? Giving the scum of the city titles like searchers of the dead and watchers of houses? Sharing the latest gossip, "So-and-so is dying, Such-and-such is dead?" Watching the bodies be buried? My God, man, you can't trust the clothes on your back!

(LAWRENCE *signs a pass.*)

BROUNKER: I'll tell them the city needs money.

LAWRENCE: I'll ask the aldermen to estimate their needs.

(BROUNKER *crosses to the desk and picks up the pass.*)

BROUNKER: How many of the aldermen did you persuade to stay?

LAWRENCE: We had a meeting together over that.

BROUNKER: Are any of them staying?

LAWRENCE: All of them are staying.

(*Pause*)

BROUNKER: Each of us to his duty, then. (*He turns to go.*)

LAWRENCE: Would you—please tell his majesty I shall do everything I can to preserve his city. Tell him we are praying for him.

BROUNKER: He will pray for you as well. You in particular, Jack. (*He exits.*)

LAWRENCE: Did you hear that, Mister Sawyer? My name in the King's prayers. Imagine that.

SAWYER: Aye, it's all who you know.... Do you want to see this sketch, Sir John?

LAWRENCE: Yes, all right.

SAWYER: I'm afraid the additional wood will be very dear.

LAWRENCE: Here we go. Disaster is a sellers' market.

SAWYER: I'm stocking all the planks I can get my hands on now, Sir.

LAWRENCE: Why on earth?

SAWYER: Well, for the coffins.

LAWRENCE: Damn it, this isn't a coffin you're building me!

SAWYER: No, Sir. Quite the opposite. (*He holds up a new sketch.*) I put the air holes in the back, away from the people you'll be meeting.

LAWRENCE: Mr Sawyer, am I going to be able to hear people through this thing?

SAWYER: Well, Sir, if I build it to specifications...no.

LAWRENCE: So people will talk and talk and they'll watch me smiling and nodding and I won't hear a word they say.

SAWYER: Very likely, Sir.

LAWRENCE: I'll be just like a politician. Thank you all the same.

SAWYER: Sir John...I have spent some time on this.

LAWRENCE: Here. Here's for your time.

(LAWRENCE *reaches into his wallet and holds out a coin.* SAWYER *hesitates.* LAWRENCE *puts the coin down on his desk.* SAWYER *covers his hand with a rag and picks up the coin.*)

SAWYER: Sir John? Good luck, Sir. (*He exits.*)

(*Pause*)

LAWRENCE: And what the hell do you want?

(*This to* GRAUNT, *who has been in the room all this time.*)

GRAUNT: Oh. Graunt. My name is John Graunt. Sir.

LAWRENCE: I suppose you want a pass out of town.

GRAUNT: Oh. No, actually. Too much to do here.

LAWRENCE: You mean you're not essential to the King?

GRAUNT: Well. Not essential, not yet. Known to him though. He made me a Fellow of the Royal Society.

LAWRENCE: Congratulations.

GRAUNT: Thank you, yes. They're all gentlemen dilettantes, really, but I'm only a tradesman, so who am I to talk. Not all dilettantes, in fairness, a few men of knowledge in there. Newton might come up with something. Do you know him, Isaac Newton, no, of course you wouldn't, promising boy, teaches maths at Cambridge, anyway, Royal Society, great honor, a year, no, two years ago, my book came out three years ago, 1662, so two years now.

LAWRENCE: And what moved his majesty to honor you?

GRAUNT: I think because I proved that if there were a plague it wouldn't be his fault.

LAWRENCE: Yes, I expect that was it.

GRAUNT: It was just a matter of looking at the Bills of Mortality.

LAWRENCE: I look at the Bills, everyone looks at the Bills.

GRAUNT: No, actually, you don't. No one does. Or did. Till me. Look. Take the plague. What does everyone think about the plague?

LAWRENCE: I find that for the most part they oppose it.

GRAUNT: You do?

LAWRENCE: Don't you?

GRAUNT: I don't see anyone preventing it, so no. Now. What does everyone think? Either that you can't predict when the plague will happen, or that it happens every twenty years like clockwork. Except for his majesty's enemies, who say that it's broken out

whenever one of his dynastic line has been crowned.
Judgment of God, you see.

LAWRENCE: And you proved his enemies wrong.

GRAUNT: I proved everybody wrong. If you really look
at the Bills, you see there've been plague years after
some coronations but not others, you see there is no
twenty-year cycle—

LAWRENCE: You see there's no predicting it.

GRAUNT: You see there is. I predicted this one.

LAWRENCE: You did?

GRAUNT: Three years ago. The plague doesn't come
from nowhere, you can see it coming months away.
Before the plague years, there is always a sickly year:
increase of fevers, increase of stillbirths, increase of
infant deaths. Same this time.

LAWRENCE: Do you know why that happens?

GRAUNT: Because everyone lies. The plague is there,
but they call it different things. Enough searchers lie,
and enough parish clerks lie—everything fine in our
parish, thank you!—and the government believes them
because it wants to, and when the rumors start, they
publish items in the *News* and the *Intelligencer* saying
it's nothing, and people believe it because they want to.
The surest symptom of the approach of the plague is a
dramatic increase in lying. Didn't you look at the Bills
last year?

LAWRENCE: Well, yes, but...

GRAUNT: You should have looked harder. (*Pause*)
Look at the Bills from the previous plagues. Where do
they start? In the parishes built on swamp land, bad
water, bad drainage, laystalls and slaughterhouses.
This plague? The same thing. They put me in the Royal
Society, so I thought they believed me, but they only

believed me about how it wouldn't be a judgment
from God on the King. I've come to ask you a favor.
Could I examine the reports from the parish clerks, the
numbers that go into the Bills of Mortality?

LAWRENCE: What are you looking for?

GRAUNT: Which direction the plague is spreading, how
fast, when it's going to arrive in any given district.

LAWRENCE: So you're a soothsayer.

GRAUNT: No. If you really look at numbers, they'll tell
you a story. But no one looks. The King doesn't even
know what he's king of.

LAWRENCE: England.

GRAUNT: But nobody knows who that is.

LAWRENCE: Can you really learn those things?

GRAUNT: If I do, will you act on it? Or would you use it
to prove that whatever happens isn't your fault?

LAWRENCE: Who's left for me to prove it to? The Lord
Mayorship was a ceremonial post, until today. Now
I'm running the place. Me, two sheriffs, a handful of
clerks and constables, every one of my aldermen, and
the goddamn Duke of Albemarle, to run the city of
London, and oh, by the bye, there's a plague.

GRAUNT: Sir John, this won't be the end of the world. If
someone stays here looking, really looking. We might
help, the next time.

LAWRENCE: And you plan to stay in London? Aren't
you afraid?

GRAUNT: What, of catching the plague? No, no, I'm just
here observing. May I look at the numbers?

LAWRENCE: Come with me. You said you were a
tradesman?

GRAUNT: Yes.

LAWRENCE: What do you call your trade?

GRAUNT: I call it statistics. Do you think it might catch on?

(LAWRENCE and GRAUNT exit as the lights crossfade to:)

Scene Three

(On the lower level: light through high windows.)

(One by one, a crowd enters.)

(THOMAS VINCENT stands on the steps, center.)

VINCENT: All of our days, until this day, we have had in our ears the whispers of God. He has murmured to us our sweetest thoughts and sung to us our dreams. And all of our days we have stopped our ears. So this day God has raised His voice, and the plague is as a roaring in the street.

To whom is God speaking? To the stricken? Some have told us that our neighbor's illness is the sign of his sin, and that the sick are greater sinners than the healthy. But when we see so many good people die, many while comforting others, can we believe this? No. The righteous die of the same disease as the most profane. We are all buried in the same grave, and sleep there together, till the morning when we rise and go our ways.

(On the lower level: Two CONSTABLES enter and stand at the back of the crowd.)

VINCENT: All of London suffers, stricken and well, and we will not suffer alone. The beauty, strength, riches of the whole kingdom lie here. So if the plague is God's sentence, it must be on the whole of our nation. And if this judgment is national, we must reason that national sins have brought it on. That there was a plague upon

the heart of this nation long before the plague upon its
body. Brothers and sisters, the constables are here.

(*The crowd turns to look at the* CONSTABLES. *No one moves
from his place.*)

CONSTABLE: Are you Thomas Vincent, formerly
minister of this parish?

VINCENT: Yes.

CONSTABLE: Will you come with us, please?

VINCENT: This congregation has asked me to speak.

CONSTABLE: You must come with us now.

(*The* CONSTABLES *take a step closer. The crowd does not
move.*)

VINCENT: Brothers and sisters, do not interfere with
these men in their duty. Do not touch them. Do not do
anything which might risk infecting them.

(*The* CONSTABLES *stop dead. Pause*)

VINCENT: If our nation were a person, could he stand
trial before the throne without terror? Has our nation
been merciful? Has our nation been charitable? Has
our nation been peaceable to its neighbors? Has it
lacked greed? Has it lacked overweening pride? What
kind of person is an empire? Is it entitled to the mercy
of God? Does it deserve—

CONSTABLE: Sir, you are under arrest!

VINCENT: Not before I finish my thought! God forgive
me, I am angry, I so wanted not to be angry by now.
So you see: Constables watch our gates, and watch our
streets, and watch our houses. But who can keep watch
over his heart, what comes in, and what goes forth?
On this day any of you may be taken under arrest by
death. I beseech you that hear these words to compare
them with the opinion of your conscience. Listen,

consider, and lay to heart. God bless you, go in peace.
Gentlemen?

(The crowd parts as VINCENT *passes through and exits.
The* CONSTABLES *follow warily. The crowd disperses as the
lights crossfade to:)*

Scene Four

(On the steps: JAMEY, *a watchman, is sitting in* SARAH's
doorway. SARAH *stands on the lower level, facing him at a
distance.)*

SARAH: I have a right to see inside my house.

JAMEY: No you don't.

SARAH: I want to see my family.

JAMEY: Won't do any good to look at them.

SARAH: I need to know they're all right.

JAMEY: Tell them to lean out the windows. As long as
they don't spit onto the street I don't mind.

SARAH: Mary! Paul! *(To* JAMEY*)* Who told the parish
my family was infected? Nobody should have said.... It
isn't true.

JAMEY: The parish hired me to watch the house, that's
all. I've watched other houses.

SARAH: Mary! Paul! Somebody! *(To* JAMEY*)* When will
you stop watching this house? When are you going to
go away?

JAMEY: When everyone inside stays healthy for two
weeks.

SARAH: Two weeks!

JAMEY: Every time another one gets sick, we have to
start the calendar again.

SARAH: That could take forever.

JAMEY: That isn't what usually happens.

SARAH: What usually happens?

JAMEY: Everybody dies.

SARAH: Mary!

(On the upper level: PAUL enters. He stands at the edge of the platform near JAMEY.)

PAUL: Sarah.

SARAH: Paul! How are they?

PAUL: They're sleeping. Everyone's fine. Mary's put the children down for the afternoon, be quiet.

SARAH: They're fine? They're all healthy?

PAUL: The doctor came, everyone's fine.

SARAH: Oh, God. Oh, thank God. Let me see them?

PAUL: They've been bouncing off the walls all day, Sarah, don't wake them up.

SARAH: Are they sleeping all right—we'd finally gotten Becca to sleep through the night, then all this—is she having nightmares? —Is Chris behaving, she promised me she'd help Mary with the little ones—is Georgie taking a bottle?

PAUL: They're eating, they're sleeping, they're fine. Really.

SARAH: *(To JAMEY)* Damn it, you, my children are in there.

JAMEY: Nice language.

SARAH: Are you going to let me in?

JAMEY: You really want to go in there? To stay?

PAUL: Sarah, don't get locked in here with us.

SARAH: What have they done, that you treat them like this?

JAMEY: They got sick.

SARAH: No.

JAMEY: They might.

SARAH: Anyone in London might be sick for Christ's sake, I might be, you might be.

JAMEY: Yes.

SARAH: So who are you keeping my family from infecting?

JAMEY: The healthy people.

SARAH: Who are the healthy people?

JAMEY: The people who pay me. You don't like the rule, talk to the aldermen.

SARAH: How much?

JAMEY: What?

SARAH: How much are you paid? I'll pay you more.

PAUL: Sarah.

JAMEY: Really?

SARAH: Yes. Tell me what you're paid. I'll double it.

JAMEY: Three watchmen were set in the stocks and beaten this week for letting people escape sick houses.

PAUL: Sarah, don't do this. The man has to live.

SARAH: What am I supposed to do?

PAUL: We need you to keep the trade going.

SARAH: There is no trade, the town's emptying out.

PAUL: Go with them, go to the trading towns.

SARAH: I can't leave the children—

PAUL: Well, you can't hang about on the street.

SARAH: They've already lost their father!

(JAMEY *edges further away from her.*)

SARAH: If I go away what if they think—I'll never see them again?

PAUL: They miss you terribly, but Mary's taking good care of them. Get out of the city, find somewhere safe to trade. If this goes on, we'll need more money to keep the children fed.

SARAH: Is this one getting what you need?

PAUL: We're eating all right. It's just the waiting.

SARAH: Don't just guard them, you turd. Keep them in food.

JAMEY: Nice with the names, thank you.

SARAH: (*To* PAUL) I have to see them. Why won't you let me see them?

PAUL: You'll only upset them. We're not supposed to get upset, the doctor said.

SARAH: You're all fine?

PAUL: Yes.

SARAH: Can I bring you anything?

PAUL: Nothing.

SARAH: You swear you're all healthy. Swear to me!

PAUL: I swear to you.

SARAH: I'll triple it. Triple your pay.

JAMEY: Would you tell her to go?

PAUL: Go, Sarah! Don't make it worse.

(*Pause*)

SARAH: Could you tell Mary—when Becca has a nightmare, if she could rub her back, sometimes it helps, and tell her—tell Mary that Georgie, if she wants to wean him to solid food that's fine because tell her I think my milk's dried up....

(Pause)

PAUL: Stay well, Sarah.

SARAH: And you. *(Pause)* Tell the children I'm well? *(She exits.)*

JAMEY: Called me a turd. Is that nice? *(He takes an apple from his pocket, examines it closely, and takes a bite.)* She's your sister, is she?

PAUL: My wife's sister.

JAMEY: Your wife talk like that?

PAUL: What *do* they pay you? *I'll* triple it. Name a price.

JAMEY: Sorry.

PAUL: Most of us are still perfectly fine.

JAMEY: If I let your family escape, I won't get a good job like this again. This is steady work. It'd be easier without the nagging, but it's steady.

PAUL: Why are you doing this to us? We've never done anything to you.

JAMEY: Before this, I used to be a day laborer. You were merchants, right?

PAUL: We were shopkeepers.

JAMEY: Indoor work, steady. You had some security.

PAUL: A little.

JAMEY: Now I've got a little security. I like it. Back in the revolution, when Cromwell was running the place, I thought that might get me some security, but it didn't. The king came back, and I thought that might do it, but it didn't. Maybe the plague will do it.

PAUL: What kind of man profits from others' misfortune?

JAMEY: Well, there's doctors, ministers, nurses, grave-diggers. Merchants. What did you sell? Candles, wasn't it?

PAUL: Yes.

JAMEY: When I burn my last candle, and I'm sitting in the dark, that's a misfortune. And there you are, with a house full of candles, ready to sell me another one. So.

(On the lower level: MRS FINCH enters, carrying her white wand.)

FINCH: *(To PAUL)* Show me the body.

(The lights crossfade to:)

Scene Five

(On the lower level: LAWRENCE's office. LAWRENCE seated, HARMAN pacing nervously.)

HARMAN: I have changed my mind!

LAWRENCE: You've what?

HARMAN: I have changed my mind, that's all. Find someone else.

LAWRENCE: There is no one else. You're the best man I have.

HARMAN: Then God help you.

LAWRENCE: Well, he isn't. What do you want to do, Edward? Leave? Go to the country?

HARMAN: Most of my patients are in Salisbury with the Court.

LAWRENCE: They won't let you into Salisbury.

HARMAN: Why won't they?

LAWRENCE: You're here. They'll be afraid of you.

HARMAN: I knew it. I've stayed here too long as it is. I'll go into the country. Give me a pass.

LAWRENCE: But what would you do in the country?

HARMAN: I would fish.

LAWRENCE: The plague is spreading into the country. You'll only find yourself in another sickroom.

HARMAN: No, I would fish, and live in a village, write about what I've seen here, pass along what I've learned, I could write something very quickly and pass it to the College. They might listen to someone who was here.

LAWRENCE: But you want to leave. You want to be here and you want to leave. Which is it?

HARMAN: I have been here. I have done more than enough for a lifetime.

LAWRENCE: What do you imagine, you'll be welcomed by your colleagues? They'll either shun you, or persuade you to admit that what you've done here is pointless, and they were right to leave.

HARMAN: It is pointless! If I administer purgatives they die, if I don't administer purgatives they die, if I keep them warm they die, if I keep them cool they die, if I lance the buboes they die in terrible pain, and if I don't then they die of the pain from the buboes.

LAWRENCE: All of them?

HARMAN: They live or die no matter what I do. There's no pattern to it. I don't think I'm giving them anything.

LAWRENCE: What do they think?

HARMAN: They keep calling for me and calling for me....

LAWRENCE: So they think you're helping them.

HARMAN: And then they die.

LAWRENCE: Or not.

HARMAN: I didn't come here to argue with you, I came here to tell you my decision and get a pass to go. You owe me that.

LAWRENCE: I do, but—

HARMAN: We shouldn't even be arguing, anger is very bad, any excitation of the spirit encourages the disease, we are supposed to remain calm and unharried.

LAWRENCE: We are supposed to live in hope.

HARMAN: Funny, isn't it? Hope, yes.

LAWRENCE: Which appears to be what your patients are getting from you.

(Pause)

HARMAN: I've almost caught it, you know. Twice that I know of. Sweats, a few spots.

LAWRENCE: Yet here you are. Alive and well.

HARMAN: I'll die here.

LAWRENCE: No.

HARMAN: "No?" Say that again, "No?" You're such a politician, John, sitting there trying to win an argument. But do you have any idea what you're asking me to do?

LAWRENCE: No. If I knew what I'm asking, and it kept me from my duty, then many more people would die. So I can't know. Can I.

(CLERK enters.)

CLERK: My Lord? The constables have brought Reverend Vincent.

LAWRENCE: Show him in.

CLERK: And the constables?

LAWRENCE: No. Alone. Thank the constables and dismiss them.

CLERK: Doctor Harman, there's a surgeon's assistant waiting outside, he says you are wanted.

HARMAN: Naturally. How many patients?

CLERK: He said patient, sir. Singular, sir.

HARMAN: Well. If it's just one. I'll see one.

CLERK: Shall I—

HARMAN: No, I'll go myself.

(CLERK *exits.* HARMAN *moves to follow him.*)

LAWRENCE: Edward. This is a pass out of town. Take it.

HARMAN: God. The first thing I do I shall walk straight into a trout stream and stand in clear water up to here and catch my weight in trout and float them all free and then I shall walk to a village where scores of women are giving birth and pull every baby out alive and tie each one a beautiful navel and the only things I shall ever touch will be mothers and newborns and water and trout.

(CLERK *enters with* VINCENT.)

LAWRENCE: May I join you there someday?

HARMAN: Yes you may. (*He takes the pass from* LAWRENCE'*s desk.*) Good luck, John.

(HARMAN *and* CLERK *exit.*)

VINCENT: Why have I been brought here?

LAWRENCE: Doctor Vincent. Do you know where you are?

VINCENT: London.

LAWRENCE: Do you know what you've done?

VINCENT: I have preached.

LAWRENCE: Do you know who I am?

VINCENT: You are the Lord Mayor.

LAWRENCE: I am the law here! It is against the law for
you to be in London. It is against the law for you to
preach. But you thought because the Court was gone,
the law was gone as well. The penalty for what you've
done is exile to the colonies.

VINCENT: With so many of my fellow dissenters? I
returned to London in the midst of the plague. Do you
seek to frighten me with a sea voyage?

LAWRENCE: Your fellows on the prison ships are dying
like flies.

VINCENT: They are dying like martyrs.

LAWRENCE: Oh, is that why you've returned here?

VINCENT: I am here because I am needed here. The
churches are open. The pulpits are empty.

LAWRENCE: And the law?

VINCENT: My parishioners tell me you are signing no
more passes. You speak to me of principles and the
law, while your friend the physician leaves with a pass
in his hand.

(Pause)

LAWRENCE: Because he'll never use it.

VINCENT: You persuaded him not to leave?

LAWRENCE: He's better than that. He persuaded
himself.

VINCENT: Perhaps you helped him to recall his better
nature. Sir John, I think we may be doing similar work.
Why do you help your friend to stay, and try to force
me to go?

LAWRENCE: He is licensed. You are not.

VINCENT: Sir John, in my time I have been licensed and unlicensed and licensed with limits and unlicensed again. I have been arrested by monarchists, who are savage, I have been arrested by Puritans, who are savager still, and now I have been arrested by you. A businessman in a sash.

LAWRENCE: Do you know what I could do to you?

VINCENT: Sir John, I've been threatened by professionals. But I am not in prison, am I. I am not on the rack. I am not on a leaking ship to nowhere. I am not dead yet. I am in the office of the Lord Mayor of London. A man who is trying to run a city with no clergy.

LAWRENCE: I don't care to argue politics with you.

VINCENT: I don't care to argue religion. You're a practical man, Sir John. I'll wager you can't tell your good Anglican doctrine from my nonconformism, and I don't expect you care.

LAWRENCE: The people I answer to can tell the difference, and they care deeply.

VINCENT: And where are they? Dancing in Salisbury? We are here. The people of London are here. In their panic, will they think, because the churchmen have gone, that God has gone as well? Once they believe that, how ever will you govern them?

LAWRENCE: Doctor Vincent, I am not the only businessman in this room.

VINCENT: Sir John, for the moment, I am simply one denomination and you are another, like francs and sterling. Tell me the rate of exchange.

(Pause)

LAWRENCE: I can't use a traitor. I won't have treason preached here.

VINCENT: Have there been false reports of my preaching?

LAWRENCE: They tell me you've said God is punishing the kingdom.

VINCENT: Am I wrong?

LAWRENCE: You can't say it. Not if you're going to keep a pulpit.

(Pause)

VINCENT: Agreed.

LAWRENCE: Do you understand me?

VINCENT: Yes, sir.

LAWRENCE: Good. Good day, then.

VINCENT: Sir John, can you do nothing for my people on the prison ships?

LAWRENCE: It's not my jurisdiction.

VINCENT: Could you speak to the Duke of Albemarle?

LAWRENCE: Oh Lord.

VINCENT: If you tell him that my people are diseased? If you tell him they are suffering frightfully?

LAWRENCE: If I tell him that they might infect his Navy. That would do it.

VINCENT: Thank you, Sir John.

LAWRENCE: Don't thank me. Say you are in my debt.

(They look at each other. The lights crossfade to:)

Scene Six

(On the lower level: Lights up as SARAH *enters, dressed for the road. She stops and looks around.)*

ROBERT: *(Off)* Excuse me!

*(*ROBERT *enters, opposite* SARAH.*)*

SARAH: Good day, sir.

ROBERT: Good day.

SARAH: Is this the way to Walthamstow?

ROBERT: Walthamstow? I don't think so. No. Probably not.

SARAH: Are you walking toward London?

ROBERT: No, no, wouldn't want to do that.

SARAH: No.

ROBERT: Are you walking from London?

SARAH: I am returning to Oxford.

ROBERT: From London?

SARAH: That general area. The outskirts. Trading.

ROBERT: This isn't the road to Oxford.

SARAH: I was afraid of that. What's the next town up this road?

ROBERT: Well. Walthamstow.

SARAH: That's what I thought. Good, if I have to be lost I'm glad to know where I am.

*(*SARAH *smiles. Nothing from* ROBERT.*)*

SARAH: Are you traveling as well?

ROBERT: No, not really.

SARAH: You live here?

ROBERT: Yes, around about here.

SARAH: Good, well, so I continue up this road to Walthamstow.

ROBERT: No, I don't think so. Probably not.

SARAH: But—

(ANDREW *and* BILL *enter.*)

SARAH: Gentlemen. Good afternoon.

BILL: May we help you, ma'am.

SARAH: Thank you, I wish to find the road through Walthamstow.

BILL: From London?

SARAH: To Oxford.

BILL: Oxford isn't this way.

ROBERT: I explained all this to her, Bill.

BILL: You're so polite nobody can understand you. Ma'am, no one passes from the London way.

SARAH: I don't understand.

BILL: There's plague in London.

SARAH: Yes, I know.

BILL: We don't want it here.

SARAH: I can understand that.

BILL: So we have to keep the infected away.

SARAH: I am pleased to hear it, I have no wish to contact infected people. May I pass, please?

ROBERT: You've come from London.

SARAH: I have been near London.

BILL: Then you've been infected.

SARAH: No.

ROBERT: Close enough.

SARAH: What?

ROBERT: You probably have.

SARAH: I say I have not.

BILL: A lot have said that. Now they're dead.

SARAH: Gentlemen, I agree with you. I want to live among healthy people. I am a healthy person. I can prove I am. And I—

ANDREW: You can prove that you're healthy.

SARAH: Thank you, sir, yes, I can. (*She rummages in her bag.*)

BILL: But Andrew—

ANDREW: You have a certificate declaring that you are healthy?

SARAH: Yes I do, I have it right here. (*She pulls it from her bag and holds it out.*)

ANDREW: Those are issued only to citizens of London. (*Pause*) You are a citizen of London, then. (*Pause*) My friends could have saved you time. People who have visited London for trade may pass through the fields. Londoners we turn back.

SARAH: Infected Londoners, of course, I understand. I'm sorry, I should have explained better, I am a good woman and not used to bargaining with men in the road as you force me to.

BILL: Not our choice.

ANDREW: And we're not bargaining. We're turning you back.

SARAH: Gentlemen, I have a certificate of health, signed by a surgeon from the College of Physicians.

ANDREW: We used to trust people with certificates, and let them through. One died in our inn, of the plague. We don't trust them anymore.

SARAH: Have some good woman examine my body for sores.

ANDREW: We've heard there's time between catching it and showing it. Why do you try to fool us with that?

BILL: There's no point arguing. The rule is made.

ANDREW: I'm explaining to her. Ma'am, this town and London, we've done good business.

SARAH: Yes, we have, I have traveled this road, gentlemen, helping in my husband's trade, I know this town, this is a good town.

ANDREW: Where's your husband now? Dead of the plague?

SARAH: Spotted fever.

ANDREW: And your children?

SARAH: My children are well.

ANDREW: In London?

SARAH: Gentlemen, please.

ANDREW: I thought as much.

BILL: Stand where you are.

ROBERT: Go back now.

ANDREW: Ma'am, we have nothing against Londoners here. Do you understand? Further up this road you'd hear talk about the sins of the city. You'd hear about comeuppance. We're not saying that. We are protecting ourselves. Once this plague is done, we want no talk in London of unfairness from here. And the next time you come, we hope to trade again.

SARAH: Please believe me, I am well.

ANDREW: You don't know, yourself. You could be standing there now, infected.

SARAH: Quarantine me. Here, by this road. I have a little money, some, enough for some food, and with your charity I can prove—

BILL: Here? Upwind of the town? Andrew, some of them say the contagion comes on the wind.

ANDREW: I'm sorry. Not here.

SARAH: Let me pass through the fields.

ANDREW: If we let Londoners through our fields, the next towns north will suspect us of infection. They'll cut us off.

BILL: We have a responsibility.

SARAH: I won't turn around here and walk back to my death, I won't do it.

BILL: You have to.

SARAH: I have to pass.

BILL: We have to stop you.

SARAH: Try!

(Pause. ROBERT *runs off.*)

SARAH: If I am infected, you wouldn't want to lay hands on me. Much better for me to pass right through your town. I'll pass through, I'll touch nothing, I'll breathe shallowly. If you try to stop me, I will throw myself into your arms. I am a good woman, I have never spoken in this way, I'm sorry.

(ROBERT *reenters. He is carrying a musket.*)

ROBERT: Ma'am? This is a musket. We will use it.

BILL: If you were a good woman, you wouldn't have brought us to this.

SARAH: Have you shot other Londoners? Where are they? Do you roll them into a ditch, what?

ROBERT: We have not.

BILL: We could.

ROBERT: Others have. In other towns.

ANDREW: Some places they've sat down in the road, like you. They've begged and starved. And gotten no explanation.

SARAH: I am not a beggar, I have never been a beggar, I have had a house and a family, we had a trade. I have children. I have three children. You don't know my name. We might be standing here a while, and you should know who I am. My name is Sarah Chandler. You see? We're alike.

ANDREW: No. Not right now. Before, and later, but not now. You have to go.

SARAH: No. I don't have to. I can stand here.

ROBERT: We'll shoot.

SARAH: All right, then.

(Pause)

ANDREW: Don't make us do this.

(SARAH takes a step toward them.)

SARAH: My husband. George. He'd have protected me. He'd have done what you're doing. He was just like you.

(SARAH takes another step. BILL steps back a pace. The others do not. SARAH peers at ROBERT, who glances away.)

ANDREW: Bill. Go get the dogs.

(BILL exits.)

ANDREW: I'm sorry, ma'am. You leave us no choice.

SARAH: No, that's all right. This road's no good to me now.

ANDREW: Thank you.

SARAH: I'm trying to get away from infection. (*She begins pacing backward, deliberately.*)

ANDREW: What are you saying? There's no infection here.

SARAH: No? Have you ever seen plague tokens? I have. (*She points at* ROBERT.) Look at him. You see that place on his neck?

ROBERT: There's nothing on my neck.

ANDREW: Of course not.

SARAH: You know best, I'm sure. Good day, gentlemen. (*She turns on her heel and exits.*)

ROBERT: We could shoot you if we wanted to! Calls herself a good woman. There's nothing on my neck.

ANDREW: Of course not.

(BILL *enters at a run.*)

BILL: There they go!

ROBERT: Scolding like a fishwife.

(*Pause*)

ANDREW: There is, though, actually. Just a little.

(ROBERT *tries to see his neck, and feels it.*)

ROBERT: What? That? Scar from a goiter, had it for years. I have.

ANDREW: Yes, of course.

BILL: What's going on?

ROBERT: It's true.

(*As they go, the lights crossfade to:*)

Scene Seven

(On the lower level: GRAUNT *enters and watches as:)*

(On the upper level: HARMAN *enters, in his protective suit. He removes it piece by piece, slowly, as if at the end of a long and exhausting day. First the head piece, then the gloves, then the cloak, then the boots. During this,* GRAUNT *turns and speaks:)*

GRAUNT: There came a time for each of us. Mine came the first time I ran a fever. When I realized I was ill, and what it might be, the sweat burst out of me. I knew it was probably nothing, but I sent for the doctor and I took to my bed and I waited to learn if I was dying. Terribly frightened. Hadn't expected that. Worth noting. I dozed, finally, and fell into a sleep. In my fever I was vouchsafed a dream.

*(*HARMAN*'s black clothing is piled at his feet by now, and he is dressed in a light shirt and trousers. During the following, he removes his shirt and examines his chest.)*

GRAUNT: I dreamed I was dying, there in my room. And a figure came to me, of a tall man, young, dressed all in linen. And I said to him, "Are you the Angel of Death?" And he said—I'll never forget—he said, "No, I asked to fetch you myself. I am the Recording Angel. Your desk is waiting. Come and help me to number the hosts of heaven."

*(*HARMAN *finds something under his arm.)*

HARMAN: Oh, Jesus. *(He frantically searches his other side.)*

GRAUNT: I woke up smiling. But I had learned. I was here.

*(*HARMAN *finds the same thing under his other arm. He feels his throat.)*

HARMAN: Oh, Jesus. Oh, Jesus.

(The lights fade quickly.)

END OF ACT ONE

ACT TWO

Scene One

(An empty stage. On the lower level: SARAH *enters, trudging, and crosses to her spot on the steps.)*

SARAH: Anybody home? *(Pause)* Mary? Paul? *(Pause)* Chris? Becca? Georgie? *(Pause)* Anybody home? *(She curls up on the steps.)*

(On the lower level: GRAUNT *enters.)*

GRAUNT: People ask me what the plague looked like. It looks like this. You wander through a crowd of absences. Friends gone, of course, but more than that. The plague is a place where you search for strangers. Where are the crowds? I don't know where I'm going without the crowds. They were my landmarks. The crowds in the morning, that was the Exchange. The crowds at noon, that was Westminster. The people milling about in the evening, that was Drury Lane. They told me I was somewhere. Where am I now? A long, open space. It used to be a street, but there's nowhere to go, and no one passes, so what is it now? A narrow meadow, where cinders bloom. All around it stand great wooden crates. They had doors and windows once, but those are nailed shut, crosses painted on them. They are crates full of poisoned air, standing in the air. You say, I don't know this place, I have to get out of here. I'll go to the fields. I'll stand in the crowds of grain, and I'll know where I am.

But when you walk to where the fields should be, the grain is gone. New hills are there, and new valleys. And this is where the crowds have gone. The surface of the earth can't hold them all and the pits are full to bursting. The people are becoming the land, and the land has broken out in sores.

I wandered around the edge of that place, where London went into the ground. I have always gone where the crowds have gone. To be alive, in this place, feels somehow like a rude mistake. Something that just isn't done anymore.

So as you walk, if you spot another living person, any other person in the world, your heart stands up, and dances. You want to run to that person, hold your heart against theirs, so your hearts can dance together. But you mustn't, you mustn't touch them, you mustn't come close to them. So you wave wildly and call out, as if you were two little boats on the high sea of the plague, unable to approach for fear the waves would crash the two of you together and you would crush each other. And this is London now: a dry sea, laced with narrow channels, hemmed in by wooden rocks full of poisoned air, where you row the little boat of your body. And now and then you see a sail on the horizon, and you wave, and it waves back, and then you take up your oars again, rowing and rowing through the ashes.

(GRAUNT *exits as the lights crossfade to:*)

(*On the lower level:* LAWRENCE *enters. He sees* SARAH, *and crosses to sit on the steps at a distance from her. He rests for a little while. She becomes aware of him and sits up, slowly.*)

LAWRENCE: What are you doing?

(*Pause*)

SARAH: This used to be my house.

LAWRENCE: What are you doing here now?

SARAH: This used to be my yard.

(Pause)

LAWRENCE: What are you doing?

SARAH: I can sit in my own yard if I want to. Why are you asking a lot of questions?

LAWRENCE: I'm supposed to be minding things around here.

SARAH: Hell of a job you're doing.

LAWRENCE: Could be worse.

SARAH: You think so? You've got quite an imagination.

(Pause)

LAWRENCE: You've lost family?

SARAH: No, I know where they are.

LAWRENCE: What are you doing here?

SARAH: Going to join them.

LAWRENCE: By sitting here?

SARAH: All you have to do is sit still and it comes to pick you up.

LAWRENCE: What does? Hackney coach?

SARAH: Death cart.

LAWRENCE: Do you feel ill? Should I get you a doctor?

SARAH: I'm all right. I was just sitting here till you came up and wanted my travel plans.

(Pause)

LAWRENCE: So you're sitting here.

SARAH: You *must* be the one in charge of this, it makes sense now.

LAWRENCE: You must be a shopkeeper's wife.

SARAH: Shopkeeper's widow.

LAWRENCE: Thought so. I'm married to one myself. Tongue like a razor. (*Pause*) My wife, remarkable, I've bought her a certain leisure, house full of servants. Me, I can sit for hours. She's got no knack for it. Just like you, I expect. She walks around, wipes this up, mends that, checks the accounts payable one more time. She's also given me a great many daughters, so she always has negotiating to do. They're in the country now.

SARAH: Lucky them.

(*Pause*)

LAWRENCE: I expect you're used to being useful. Come on.

SARAH: Where?

LAWRENCE: Anywhere. Lots to do.

SARAH: My house is closed. Our shop is shut. My family's dead. My work is all done.

LAWRENCE: Big house, London. Big shop. I used to sit in meetings, now there's no people to meet with so I walk around. I walk around London like a housewife now, saying, "What else needs doing? There must be something else to do." And there always is. Interesting way to live.

(LAWRENCE *stands and takes some scraps of paper from his wallet. He shuffles through them, takes one and lays it on the ground between himself and* SARAH.)

LAWRENCE: So. Go here first.

(SARAH *looks at the piece of paper.*)

SARAH: I've got my ride coming.

LAWRENCE: Go here first. Two streets down, turn left, third house. There's a woman sick, in childbed. She won't survive, neither will the baby.

SARAH: What do you want me to do about it?

LAWRENCE: Everything you can. I expect that's a lot.

SARAH: No.

LAWRENCE: I expect it's more than you know. Now.
Doctor Harman will be coming to check on them this
afternoon. Tell him I sent you. After they're dead,
report to him. There's food and a bit of money. Enough
to keep body and soul together.

SARAH: Mine aren't on the best of terms.

LAWRENCE: Comes of sitting still. There's the address.

*(LAWRENCE exits. SARAH looks at the piece of paper as the
lights crossfade to:)*

Scene Two

*(On the lower level: Lights up as LAWRENCE'S CLERK
enters, carrying a set of tongs with very long handles and a
large leather portfolio. BROUNKER'S CLERK enters, carrying
a flaming brazier of coals, which he sets between them.)*

LAWRENCE'S CLERK: Morning.

BROUNKER'S CLERK: Morning. How's London?

LAWRENCE'S CLERK: Worse. Tim Bishop died.

BROUNKER'S CLERK: I liked him.

*(BROUNKER'S CLERK exits. LAWRENCE'S CLERK looks
back over his shoulder and checks quickly in his portfolio.
BROUNKER'S CLERK reenters carrying his own set of long-
handled tongs and portfolio.)*

BROUNKER'S CLERK: Yours coming?

LAWRENCE'S CLERK: Yeah. Yours waiting?

BROUNKER'S CLERK: Yeah.

LAWRENCE'S CLERK: Shit.

(GRAUNT *enters hurriedly, carrying a large sheaf of papers.*)

GRAUNT: Is this the place?

LAWRENCE'S CLERK: Yes, sir. Have you seen him?

GRAUNT: No, haven't you?

LAWRENCE'S CLERK: Look sharp.

(BROUNKER *enters. Everyone bows.*)

BROUNKER: Do you have the Bill of Mortality?

LAWRENCE'S CLERK: Yes, my Lord.

BROUNKER: I shall examine it.

LAWRENCE'S CLERK: My Lord, I expect he'll be along in a very few moments. (*During the following, he takes a large sheet of paper from his portfolio, lays it carefully on the ground, and picks it up with his set of tongs.*) He is often out of the office, my Lord, and the bells ring so often for the d...for so many things. It is difficult to tell the time.

GRAUNT: Lord Brounker, it is good to see you again. Graunt—

BROUNKER: Mister Graunt, yes—

GRAUNT: John Graunt, we have met, if you—when I was accepted into the Royal Society?

BROUNKER: Ah, yes.

GRAUNT: And then again, it would have been a year ago, no, November last, and here it is only July, is it only eight months, how slowly the year is going. Eight months ago—

BROUNKER: At a Royal Society meeting.

GRAUNT: How kind of you to remember, yes, the session at which Mr Clarke and Mr Pearse fed opium to the greyhound.

BROUNKER: Most informative, yes.

(During this exchange, LAWRENCE'S CLERK, *using his tongs, holds the piece of paper out to* BROUNKER'S CLERK, *who receives it in his set of tongs and holds it in the smoke of the brazier before holding it out to* BROUNKER, *who takes it and examines it.)*

GRAUNT: Sir John asked me to come along today to present some observations I have made with regard to the Bills of Mortality, that is the most recent—

BROUNKER: This is frightful.

GRAUNT: Yes. But its true significance is only revealed in relation to the others, which I—

*(*LAWRENCE *enters, a bit winded.)*

LAWRENCE: Good day, my Lord. Did I keep you waiting?

BROUNKER: Good day, Sir John. I was not waiting.

LAWRENCE: The Court's move from Salisbury to Oxford went smoothly?

BROUNKER: Thank you, yes. There was some concern over Lady Castlemayne, who is very near her time to be traveling, but all went bravely.

LAWRENCE: London salutes them. The King is well?

BROUNKER: Quite well. *(Pause)* It is good to see you looking so well.

LAWRENCE: I *am* well.

BROUNKER: That is good. I have examined the Bill of Mortality for the week. Your losses are frightful.

LAWRENCE: Yes, they are. As I have asked Mister Graunt here to explain. Have you met?

BROUNKER: Yes, we've known each other quite some time.

LAWRENCE: Graunt?

(GRAUNT *kneels and spreads out his sheets of paper on the ground as he speaks.*)

GRAUNT: As you can see, the plague is flowing eastward.

BROUNKER: Yes.

GRAUNT: Parishes close to the center of London are reporting many more cases than last week, and even the most eastern suburbs now have a few.

BROUNKER: But the west is improving. The cases are fewer.

GRAUNT: So are the people. You can see that all deaths are fewer there, from all causes, but higher in the east. The people are moving eastward, taking the plague along with them.

BROUNKER: Can they be stopped?

GRAUNT: They should have been, yes, by taking care of them where they were. Look at the pattern. The losses were always worst in the most overcrowded districts.

BROUNKER: Yes...

GRAUNT: Now we see that pattern, the exact pattern, duplicated in districts that once had light and space and air. The people ran away to healthy neighborhoods and crowded into them and now they bear the same numbers as the most teeming slums. Do you see? The number of losses is rising, and not only the number of losses, but the speed at which the losses rise, and not only the speed at which they rise, but the speed at which the rise is rising. The rate of acceleration, you see?

BROUNKER: Ah, yes.

GRAUNT: Do you see?

BROUNKER: You may have lost me toward the end there.

GRAUNT: Look at the Bills! Turn the pages week by week, you see a great wave of numbers sweeping across London, spilling here, eddying there, stagnating and deepening—

LAWRENCE: Thank you, Mister Graunt.

GRAUNT: (*On his knees among his papers*) It's all here. Anyone can see it.

BROUNKER: Most informative. (*He nods and turns away.*)

GRAUNT: It's all...right here.

BROUNKER: Sir John, are the regulations being enforced?

LAWRENCE: Insofar as we are able. Enforcement requires healthy enforcers, and there are very few of them left. Especially given the wages.

BROUNKER: Is the nation's charity not sufficient?

LAWRENCE: They give little, which lengthens the emergency, so they give even less. We had hoped the Court might respond.

BROUNKER: We have done so.

(BROUNKER'S CLERK *takes a large piece of vellum from his portfolio and, using his tongs, passes it to* LAWRENCE'S CLERK, *who takes it in his tongs and passes it to* LAWRENCE, *who stares at it, during the following.*)

BROUNKER: The King has proclaimed a monthly fast day on which collections will be taken at churches across the country. There is the list of subscribers. You'll see his majesty's signature, encouragingly large.

LAWRENCE: But the Privy Council sends no money.

BROUNKER: The Council has the defense of the nation to consider. According to our intelligence reports, the Dutch believe we are powerless in the grip of this disease and are preparing what they hope will be a death blow against our shipping. What about the Poor Rate?

LAWRENCE: We have great trouble collecting the Poor Rate from the landholders, because they have abandoned the city. Even if we could it would be too little.

GRAUNT: Half the remaining households are infected.

LAWRENCE: My supply lines for food are down to a trickle.

BROUNKER: Sir John—

LAWRENCE: There are almost no pest houses, those are full, and so dangerous that many would rather die alone than be taken there. We need more death carts, more sea coal for fires to purge the air, new graves must be dug, the laystalls are polluting the drinking water, garbage rots in the streets—

BROUNKER: Jack. There is not enough money in the entire Exchequer to supply all of these.

LAWRENCE: Supply *one*. Any *one*.

BROUNKER: These needs are desperate, but this is a desperate time. You knew it would be so as well as we. All you pledged was to keep the situation in control. Are you reporting that the situation is out of your control?

LAWRENCE: No, I am not reporting that, but—

BROUNKER: I ask merely because you seem, perhaps, overscheduled.

LAWRENCE: I am certainly undermanned.

(*Pause*)

BROUNKER: The city is lacking certain essentials. I will make this known.

*(*BROUNKER *crosses up the steps to the upper level.*
LAWRENCE *pursues him.)*

LAWRENCE: No one will trade with us. No one will
allow us to leave the city. Whole areas of the Isles—all
of Scotland forbids any Londoner even to cross the
border. We are pariahs in our own country. How are
we to live?

BROUNKER: I will make this known. I will make all of
this known.

LAWRENCE: It is known. Everyone knows our trouble,
that is why we are shunned. Make it felt.

(The lights crossfade to:)

Scene Three

(On the lower level: FINCH *is sprawled on the floor at a
distance from the cot. She tries to put weight on her legs. She
moans, and stops. She wipes her face on her shoulder.)*

FINCH: Stupid cow. Try the arms. *(She tries putting
weight on her arms and yells at the pain.)* Jesus *Christ!*
Better. Off we go. *(Balling her fists, she plants them on
the floor ahead of her. She takes a deep breath and pulls
herself forward. She breathes for a moment, then pulls herself
forward. Then she loses her nerve and sinks back.)* All right,
Lizabeth. Doctor sees you can't walk, you're a goner.
(She gathers herself.) Bet you can't get into bed before
he comes. *(She hauls herself forward three times.)* Jesus
Christ Jesus *Christ* Jesus *Christ!* *(She collapses, panting.)*
I am not cursing. I am praying. *(She gets up on her fists
again.)* Elizabeth Finch. You can do this. Three more
steps. *(She shuts her eyes and pulls herself forward.)* Come
on, Lizabeth. Two more. *(She pulls herself forward.)* Poor
little Lizzie. One more step to Mama.

(She pulls herself forward and opens her eyes. She is a few feet shy of the bed. She reaches out and touches the frame, a long stretch away. She leans her head on her arm and cries.)

SARAH: *(Off)* Is anyone up there!

(FINCH looks up, fearful.)

FINCH: *(In a hoarse whisper)* Here.

SARAH: *(Off)* Is anyone up there!

(FINCH grabs the edge of the bed with both hands. Too quickly to change her mind, she drags herself into the bed.)

FINCH: Yaaaah! *(She sits in the bed, her breathing ragged and deep.)* I win.

(SARAH enters, carrying a bag.)

FINCH: Sarah. Well, now. Good of you to call.

SARAH: Mrs Finch. You're ill.

FINCH: Been better, been better. When you called, I thought you were a nurse down there. Doctor's coming any moment, you see, so I don't know how long I'll be able to—

SARAH: He'll be along.

(SARAH pulls a set of leather straps from the bag and tosses them to FINCH. Each strap has a loop at one end.)

SARAH: Wrists and ankles.

FINCH: You're the nurse?

(SARAH takes a pair of gloves from the bag and sets them aside.)

FINCH: Since when?

SARAH: Days now. Wrists and ankles.

(FINCH loosely straps one ankle to the frame of the cot. SARAH pulls a kerchief and a small bottle of spirits from the bag. During the following, she soaks the cloth in the spirits.)

FINCH: I was sorry to hear about your family.

(SARAH *looks at her.*)

FINCH: I wish I could have done even more to help.

SARAH: Other ankle.

FINCH: I, ah...the sores.

SARAH: Where.

(FINCH *points to her groin, both sides.*)

SARAH: Just around the ankle, then.

(FINCH *puts the strap around the other ankle and lets the loose end dangle.* SARAH *ties the cloth over her own mouth and nose and puts the gloves on.*)

FINCH: Do you know who's been doing my job the last few days? Must be a hell of a backlog. Have you—seen a lot of cases?

(SARAH *crosses to kneel next to* FINCH *without ever touching her.* FINCH *hesitates, then puts her wrists in the loops of the straps.*)

SARAH: Arms to your sides.

(FINCH *does so, and* SARAH *winds the strap of one wrist around the bed frame and ties it.*)

FINCH: Sarah?

(SARAH *silences her with a look. As* FINCH *watches,* SARAH *crosses to the other side and does the same to the other wrist.*)

FINCH: I know you, Sarah. You're a good girl.

(FINCH *is leaning up on her elbows.* SARAH *kneels next to the unbound ankle.*)

FINCH: Sarah. The children barely suffered at all.

(SARAH *looks at* FINCH *expressionlessly, takes the dangling end of the strap and winds it once around the bed frame.*)

FINCH: They went in their sleep. All of them. They looked so peaceful.

(They look at each other. SARAH *pulls the strap tight, forcing* FINCH's *legs apart.* FINCH *chokes back a scream. They stay like that for a long moment.)*

HARMAN: *(Off)* Elizabeth Finch?

FINCH: Eeyyesss!

*(*SARAH *stands as* HARMAN *enters, carrying his headpiece.* VINCENT *follows him.)*

HARMAN: Running late. How is she?

FINCH: Get her out of here!

SARAH: Delirious.

FINCH: You—!

HARMAN: Buboes?

SARAH: In the groin.

HARMAN: Ah huh... *(He puts on his headpiece and prepares to examine her.)*

FINCH: Wait! No!

HARMAN: Lie still.

*(*HARMAN *bends over* FINCH *and begins his examination. She cannot help but gasp in pain. He straightens up.)*

HARMAN: I thought as much.

FINCH: *(To* VINCENT*)* You! Please! Give me something.

VINCENT: I am not the physician.

FINCH: *(To* HARMAN*)* I don't want you yet! *(To* VINCENT*)* You, the minister.

*(*HARMAN *moves to go.)*

HARMAN: Fine. I have too many other patients.

VINCENT: *(To* HARMAN*)* Where are you going?

HARMAN: If she thinks I can't help her, I can't do a thing. My other patients don't know I can't help them, so I might be able to fool them into getting well.

(FINCH *moans.*)

VINCENT: You can't leave her.

HARMAN: The buboes in her groin have hardened and are eating into her vitals. Unless I lance them, the pain will continue until she dies.

FINCH: No! He wants to spade it out of me!

HARMAN: She knows, you see. If I lance them, I may kill her with the pain.

VINCENT: Stay a few minutes.

HARMAN: The nurse will stay.

FINCH: No! Not the nurse!

VINCENT: You have to do something, you're here to do something, so do it! Otherwise why are you here?

HARMAN: I don't know! Why are you? (*Pause. To* SARAH:) Prepare the instruments, Mrs Chandler.

(SARAH *lays out several horrific devices during the following.*)

FINCH: (*To* VINCENT) Give me something!

HARMAN: (*To* VINCENT) Go ahead. Show me how it's done.

VINCENT: How may I help you, good woman?

FINCH: Give me something.

VINCENT: What?

FINCH: Blessing, penance, absolution, something. I've been a sinner, led into sin, this one here for one—

SARAH: Me?

VINCENT: This woman wishes you to recover.

FINCH: No! They've tempted me with bribes, they used my need, the parish, the aldermen—

VINCENT: The parish led you into sin?

FINCH: They hire sinners, anyone with a job like mine, they think our souls are damned already, but they're wrong, aren't they?

VINCENT: Of course they are. It is good your trial leads you to these thoughts.

FINCH: I repent my yielding to their temptations.

VINCENT: Then you shall be saved.

FINCH: Bless you, bless you—

VINCENT: For your salvation to be complete, you must forgive her.

(Pause)

FINCH: Sarah? *(Spat like a curse)* Forgive you.

SARAH: *(A curse back)* Forgive you, too.

HARMAN: Shall we begin?

FINCH: *(To* VINCENT*)* Have you done it? My salvation.

VINCENT: Yes.

FINCH: All right. As long as that's fixed up.

VINCENT: God keep you all, then.

HARMAN: Where are you going?

VINCENT: I have many other parishioners to see.

HARMAN: Last rites may be called for, save yourself a trip. Unless you feel they're unnecessary, after such a deeply convincing repentance.

(Pause)

VINCENT: We do what we can with what we're given. God has to know that. He is not an idiot.

SARAH: (*Very quietly, to no one*) Why's He doing this, then.

(HARMAN *takes an instrument and bends over* FINCH.)

HARMAN: Would you pray for me, too? I don't feel well at all.

(FINCH *screams bloody murder.*)

(*The lights crossfade to:*)

Scene Four

(*On the upper level: Lights up on* GRAUNT.)

GRAUNT: And here, I confess it, there is a gap in my account.

People ask me, "Did you...lose anyone? Did anyone close to you..." Die, is what they mean. And that question, that question...is not their fault. They weren't there, you see. As I was. They're not...here. Always. Did you lose anyone. Who died.

In the month of June, we lost a thousand people to the plague. In the month of July, we lost a thousand people every week. In the month of August, we lost a thousand people every day. And one day, after all the deaths that had gone before, and with everyone gone from the city who could, with so few of us left alive, one day, toward summer's end, we lost a thousand every hour.

You have to understand: We did not know this at the time. All we knew...all we knew was that the sun was very hot. From dawn onwards it was a noontime sun, at a steeper and steeper angle, unblinking, until it stood in the center of the sky and that was all we knew, that the sun was very hot, and there was nowhere we could go and not hear screaming.

I say we lost a thousand every hour, but it was
probably more, for that day...that was the day we lost
count of ourselves. And what we did, what we must
have done to be among those still alive by the end of
that day, none of us can tell. We became a different
species, without the power to speak to you. And then
we were human again, but with no words for what we
must have done.

On that day, everyone in London died. All of us.

Some of us...came back.

But with a gap in our accounts.

But this must be part of what I tell you, as your guide
to this place, like our cartographers, who, in the places
of which no description is possible, can only write:
"Here There Be Tygers."

(The lights crossfade to:)

Scene Five

*(On the lower level: HARMAN and SARAH enter, he in his
protective suit, she carrying the bag of gear. SARAH gets a
quizzical look on her face, and stops. HARMAN notices she is
no longer beside him, and turns. Her eyes are shut, and she
is smiling.)*

HARMAN: Mrs Chandler?

SARAH: Oh, that's lovely.

HARMAN: Mrs Chandler. Are you well.

(SARAH opens her eyes and points at HARMAN's headpiece.)

SARAH: Oh, take that thing off.

(HARMAN pulls off the headpiece.)

HARMAN: I had forgotten I had it on, if you can— Oh.
A breeze. Oh my—

SARAH: Mm.

HARMAN: When was the last time I felt the air moving.

(SARAH *opens her hands in the breeze and chortles with helpless pleasure.* HARMAN *takes off his gloves.*)

HARMAN: God knows where it's been.

SARAH: I do not care.

(HARMAN *sniffs the air, first tentatively, then deeply.*)

HARMAN: What is that.... Straw?

SARAH: Fresher. Hay.

HARMAN: New-mown hay.

SARAH: Somewhere someone is mowing hay.

HARMAN: A man with a scythe.

SARAH: What does it—

HARMAN: —remind you of?

(HARMAN *and* SARAH *breathe the air hungrily.*)

SARAH: I'm getting a bit light-headed.

HARMAN: Be careful.

SARAH: Funny. I've lived in London my whole life, and never been here.

HARMAN: This district?

SARAH: The middle of the street. Only at a run, looking out for carriages. Worth your life to stand this long, before. Feels a bit wicked. If this ever ends, and I survive, I should like to stand perfectly still for a very long time.

HARMAN: It's dying down.

SARAH: Come back! Come— !

(*The breeze picks up again.* HARMAN *and* SARAH *smile.*)

HARMAN: Ha! Well done!

(SARAH *shuts her eyes and bathes her arms in the wind.* HARMAN *looks around him, and down.*)

HARMAN: This was one of the busiest streets in London. Look at it. Grass is growing.

SARAH: Who does it remind me of...oh....

(SARAH's *voice trails away, and she breathes in the scent of the air. She chuckles, quiet and deep. She opens her eyes.* HARMAN *is staring at her. He glances away and she looks down. Pause*)

HARMAN: There it goes.

SARAH: There it goes.

HARMAN: Mrs Chandler, I— there's something I would like to ask you, but—well, it is awkward.

SARAH: Please.

HARMAN: Well, as you may have noticed, I have not been as strong in the last few days as I have been, and with that and some other signs, I think it is clear that I am...not well.

SARAH: I'm sorry.

HARMAN: It is probably a mild case, really, and I have survived before, it is probably nothing very much, really, just a quite minor case of the bubonic plague. (*He hears what he's said, and bursts out laughing.*) When I think of the things I used to worry about.

SARAH: You wanted to ask me something.

HARMAN: I've seen what happens to people...later in this. Many become delirious. Some run into the street. In their fever they can infect others.

SARAH: I've never seen that happen.

HARMAN: None of my patients has, because we bind them firmly. But I've seen them struggle.

SARAH: Perhaps they just don't want to be tied up.

HARMAN: Of course not, but they have to be. I'm afraid that when the fever comes upon me, I might escape. I can't have that. I've worked very hard against this disease, and I won't be responsible for spreading it. I'm afraid of what I might do, when I'm not in my right mind.

SARAH: You want me to bind you to a bed?

HARMAN: Yes, but I'm stronger than you, so that may not hold me. Now listen to me please. I know that sometimes you nurses will wait until a patient is asleep, loot his valuables, and abandon him to die alone.

SARAH: I never.

HARMAN: I've heard you do.

SARAH: Me?

HARMAN: Nurses in general.

SARAH: Have you seen this?

HARMAN: I've heard it said, by gentlemen whose word I trust.

SARAH: Of course, then, you know best.

HARMAN: Now. I have an arrangement to suggest. I shall tell you, before I die, an inventory of my most valuable possessions. Some you would not recognize nor know where to find without my help. I shall relate these to you in order of increasing value. It will be well worth your time. In exchange you will stay by me, and watch for signs that I am no longer myself. Now. I also know that you nurses will sometimes grow tired of waiting and smother your patients.

SARAH: I—

HARMAN: I say I have heard many stories of this. When I begin to struggle, I want you to smother me. I gather you know how to do it in such a way that there is little danger of detection. Two wet cloths, one laid over the other, covering my mouth and nose. And sit upon my chest if that seems called for.

SARAH: You medical men have a very low opinion of nurses.

HARMAN: Mrs Chandler. I am not blaming you. It's wrong, but the times are wrong, and if we are to survive we must act as the times permit. Do you agree?

SARAH: I have not been nursing long, sir. Perhaps a more experienced nurse would be more skilled at this operation.

HARMAN: There are very few nurses left alive. By the time you find one, it may be too late. Listen. With what I'll give you, you won't have to nurse anymore to survive. You are alone in the world. A widow.

SARAH: Yes, Sir.

HARMAN: In a desperate city, with no support, nothing for comfort? What else could you have done?

SARAH: When my husband was alive, I used an accurate scale. I kept true accounts. From the hour of his death I've been treated like a thief.

HARMAN: Mrs Chandler, I—

SARAH: They wouldn't even let me out of London, I think they would have shot me, but I said, if you think I have the plague and you shoot me, then what will you do? I'll still have the plague, but I'll be dead in the middle of your road.

HARMAN: Good for you.

SARAH: So they set the dogs on me. I ran down the road with the dogs snapping at me until they called them back. Then they whipped the dogs into the ditch and shot them.

HARMAN: Why?

SARAH: They had touched me, the dogs. I heard one of the men crying. One of the dogs must have been a favorite of his. I'm standing in the road a quarter mile back toward London and I can hear the man crying over his dog. And all for nothing, I wasn't sick, I told them I wasn't—

HARMAN: Where was this?

SARAH: Walthamstow, a month ago.

HARMAN: The plague is in Walthamstow now.

SARAH: Good!

(HARMAN *looks at* SARAH. *She turns away. Long pause.*)

HARMAN: You came back here and nursed the sick. Why?

SARAH: I was hungry.

HARMAN: It was brave and good of you.

SARAH: I was a shopkeeper's wife, sick people are the only commodity now.

HARMAN: It was good of you.

(Pause)

SARAH: Most of the doctors left long ago. Why did you stay?

HARMAN: I had no choice either.

SARAH: Why not?

HARMAN: I have my own dogs, to set on myself. (*He touches his head.*) I kennel them here. (*He starts to walk again.*) We should be on our way. Where's the next patient?

SARAH: Are you sure you want me to do what you asked?

HARMAN: Yes. Will you do it?

SARAH: I'll stay with you.

HARMAN: And the other?

(The lights crossfade to:)

Scene Six

(On the lower level: GRAUNT *and* LAWRENCE *enter, in conversation.)*

GRAUNT: I was visiting the offices of Cripplegate parish, I wanted to check on what I suspected was some terrible underreporting. The office was locked, in the middle of the day, I called, no answer, I found a sexton, we broke in, and there was the parish clerk, at his desk, parish register on his desk, his head on the parish register.

LAWRENCE: Dead? Of the plague.

GRAUNT: In the middle of making an entry. I told the sexton to go for a doctor, he said the man was dead, we needed a searcher, I ordered him to go for a doctor, I was very upset, I didn't know why, I hadn't known the man. The sexton went for help, and I stood there, looking. I should have left the room, but I couldn't help looking.

LAWRENCE: At a corpse? You must have had your fill of—

GRAUNT: At the ledger. He'd been underreporting, and now I understood why, he must have been ill, so I wanted to see his numbers. I could see on the open page, almost the last thing he'd written. I was peering around his head. There was ink on his cheek. The entry for plague read 504.

LAWRENCE: My God. For one parish? For one week?

GRAUNT: I stood there thinking, 504. Yes, terrible. But. Did he count himself?

LAWRENCE: Graunt.

GRAUNT: I stood there, thinking that. May I tell you something? You have been so open to my information.

LAWRENCE: It has been of help. It will be in the future as well.

GRAUNT: Yes, so I think it's important that you know this. You see, I have always followed the trends. And death is so much the rage now. Sometimes the plague so infects my mind that I begin to think, all right, perhaps the world would not be worse off, with fewer people. Not excluding myself in this, not by any means. Each of us is a loose end, really. I know what a sinful thought this is. I put it down quickly. But the thought returns. I think of the world as a great equation, a problem whose solution I pursue with too much impatience. So many wretched sufferers, and their suffering children, on and on. Whole groups of people would simplify matters considerably if they would just disappear. I think this! And then I remember how I yearn for people who think like me to govern the world. What if someone like me were in charge of things, and yielded to this thought? I wonder if I'm doing a dangerous thing. I wonder...if almost anything can become a plague. I just thought you should keep it in mind. For the future.

LAWRENCE: I will.

GRAUNT: I stood there a long time, I think. Thinking. The sexton came back, without a doctor, and I asked him why, and he told me the doctor was dead.

LAWRENCE: What doctor?

GRAUNT: Edward Harman, did you know him?

(Pause)

LAWRENCE: Yes. I did, yes. He was my fr.... He was my physician. In fact. (Pause) Is there to be a funeral?

GRAUNT: Funerals are forbidden.

LAWRENCE: Do you know where the funeral is to be?

GRAUNT: Yes. I went there for the burial of the clerk.

LAWRENCE: Would you take me there?

GRAUNT: Yes.

LAWRENCE: Thank you. I would count it a favor.

GRAUNT: I would rather not hear the word "count."

(*They cross up the steps and exit as the lights crossfade to:*)

Scene Seven

(*On the lower level: A few people enter, one by one, including* LAWRENCE *and* GRAUNT. SARAH *enters quickly, looking from one face to another. She sees* LAWRENCE *and goes to him.*)

SARAH: Sir. You're the Lord Mayor, aren't you?

LAWRENCE: Yes.

SARAH: You hired me.

LAWRENCE: I remember. I sent you to work with Doctor Harman.

SARAH: Yes. I have a message for you.

LAWRENCE: From Doctor Harman? Did you nurse him as well?

SARAH: Before he went unconscious, he'd asked me to get him some wet cloths, and I was standing next to the bed, and.... And I'd thought I'd be able do it. He'd started to suffer, and I've seen so much of that, and he had asked me, but—

LAWRENCE: I don't understand, what had he asked you to do?

SARAH: He'd asked me to help him. Toward the end. I
stood there next to the bed, but it was very hard for me
to bring myself to do it, he must have seen how hard it
was, all of a sudden one of his hands started grabbing
at my wrist, his arm was tied down and he still
made the reach, and I said, I'm trying to do it, Doctor
Harman, he was panting for breath, the sores were in
his throat, he couldn't get a word out, he took my wrist
and drew a line across it with his finger, and another,
and another, and I said, what do you want from me,
and he drew a line between and then he drew a steeple
and a funnel and a comb and what he was doing was
spelling out I HAVE CHANGED MY MIND. (*Pause*)
He lived for two days after that. It was very hard. But
he was calmer toward the end, and he wrote on a slate.
It took a long time. But what he said was to tell the
Lord Mayor that he stayed. That he stayed the whole
time.

(*Pause*)

LAWRENCE: You stayed there a long while, didn't you?
Nursing him.

SARAH: A fair while, yes, Sir.

LAWRENCE: How do you feel?

SARAH: I'm a little tired. I think I'm going to rest here a
while.

LAWRENCE: Thank you. Thank you for the message.

(*VINCENT enters on the upper level, and stops at the sight of
the crowd. They turn toward him.*)

VINCENT: So. Here we are again. And so many. I came,
every day I come, expecting to find no mourners left
but myself. Sir John. Oh yes of course, he was a friend
of yours. Shall we begin? I shall say a few words about
Edward Harman and lead you in prayer. I should
repeat that it is dangerous for you to be here. This

place breathes infection. I confess I have wondered
why we keep coming. But here we are, so let us begin,
I should speak of Edward and recount his life.... Am I
the only one who wonders why we come here? Why
we keep on grieving?

Consider it. Nothing in the world eats the heart so
much as grief. Love is such a powerful thing, that
if it places any object in our hearts, we can scarcely
bear it to be taken from us, without tearing our hearts
in pieces. But still we can grieve. What gives us the
strength? And think what we are asking when we
grieve. What is the hope hidden in mourning? That
our friend not be lost to us. That he breathe the living
air, and join us again, for friendship's sake. That
something, anything, rise from the dead. Yet we know
this cannot happen. So why have we come?

If I could tell you some event of Edward's life and
say, "This. This is how he became good...." But we
never will know that. So what is left to say of him? He
worked here. He kept to his work. But I have already
said this of hundreds....

Perhaps we should pray. Many have lost their faith
by now, very many, the risen God was our hope, and
hope is hard to recollect, like so many of our friends, so
many burials, they blur together, all the dead.... But let
us pray now, let us speak to God, shall we, of what is
in our hearts. If we dare to speak such things.

Lord...what are we to do?

When the plague began, we thought we knew what
you meant. We thought you were correcting us. So we
tried to correct each other. We were wrong. What do
you want of us now? Do you want us to acknowledge
this world to be a hollow thing? Sir, we acknowledge
it. We have learned what lies in our hollow places, we
have smelt the corruption there. Are you punishing
us? If so, then you know that we are punished now

beyond our comprehension. Only a tyrant punishes the helpless beyond their comprehension. You know this.

We do not know what you want!

We gather in this graveyard every day. Today for Edward Harman, tomorrow for any of us. We no longer know why. But each day more die, we come out to the edge of the city and leave them here, we pray to you and go in again, and more die, and we come out here, and go in once more, and come out, and go in, and come out, and go in, it is unthinking, it is regular, it is constant. Like breathing.

Like the breath...

As if *we* were the breath of some great...living being....

Which has risen.

Brothers and sisters. Look at yourselves? Look what we have been made?

Go in peace.

(VINCENT *goes. Some of the crowd disperse.* GRAUNT *watches.* SARAH *is sitting on the steps. On the lower level,* BROUNKER *enters.*)

BROUNKER: Sir John! The most excellent news! Lady Castlemayne is delivered of a splendid boy. The King has acknowledged him, and named him Duke of Northumberland. The Court rejoices! In the midst of death, we are in life!

LAWRENCE: All of London salutes his majesty.

BROUNKER: I shall report it so.

LAWRENCE: And while you do, report this as well. If I do not receive the Poor Rate from any wealthy person, I shall instruct the constables to open his house and seize his property.

(Pause)

BROUNKER: You wouldn't.

LAWRENCE: Either I shall do it or the poor will do it.

BROUNKER: We will call out the army.

LAWRENCE: The army has the plague.

BROUNKER: You are a man of duty, Jack. You swore to do your utmost to preserve the city. Now you permit the city to be looted?

LAWRENCE: The city charter grants the Lord Mayor the power to collect the rates.

BROUNKER: I will report on this meeting to the court.

LAWRENCE: Do so. Please.

BROUNKER: Its information, but not its tone. The court well knows you are doing a hero's labor, a Herculean labor. Intemperance is permitted in our heroes.

LAWRENCE: Report whatever will make them act.

BROUNKER: Jack. Consider what you are doing. If you do this, if you strip the great houses to appease the poor, what becomes of your pledge to the King to preserve London?

(LAWRENCE *looks at* BROUNKER, *and at* GRAUNT.)

LAWRENCE: Sir, you may tell the King that my idea of what constitutes London has greatly changed.

(LAWRENCE *turns and exits.* BROUNKER *watches him, then turns and exits the opposite way.* GRAUNT *starts to follow* LAWRENCE, *and stops.*)

GRAUNT: Excuse me. Ma'am? Excuse me. We should go.

SARAH: Yes.

GRAUNT: It isn't safe to stay here, the smell is unhealthy.

SARAH: My family is here. (*Pause*) No one asks what happened to people, anymore.

GRAUNT: I do, actually. It's part of what I do.

SARAH: Why?

GRAUNT: I work with the Bills of Mortality.

SARAH: But they're wrong.

GRAUNT: Yes, I know.

SARAH: My husband didn't die of spotted fever.

(Pause)

GRAUNT: Shouldn't we go?

(Pause)

SARAH: I can't stand up.

GRAUNT: I'll get some help. Shall I get some help?

SARAH: We already buried the doctor. Now that he's dead—would you believe it? I think I'm the only person I know. Strange feeling. Like floating in the ether. *(Pause)* I don't feel well at all. *(Pause)* My name is Sarah Chandler, my husband's name was George Chandler, he died in Cripplegate parish, third of June. You could check the records, you could correct it. Anyone put down with spotted fever, smallpox. When they began punishing people for having the plague, we had to die of other things.

GRAUNT: I appreciate your telling me, Mrs Chandler.

SARAH: Well. You're trying to keep an inventory. I've kept inventory. *(Pause)* What's your name?

GRAUNT: Graunt. John Graunt, actually, if you— Fellow of the Royal Society.

SARAH: I'm pleased to meet you, Mr Graunt. You should leave now.

GRAUNT: Are you certain?

SARAH: I'll rest here for a while.

(GRAUNT *looks at her for a moment. He turns, and looks up.*)

GRAUNT: We knew so little. And we don't know much. So people ask me if we learned anything during the plague.

And I say we did. Newton did. He came up with something, just as I said, and he taught it to us. Those of us who lived. Plague spread to Cambridge, you see, and it closed for the duration, everyone scattered. Newton found himself on a lonely country estate. Nothing to do but take walks and think. One day, he walked in an apple orchard, noticed an apple fall to the earth.

Have you heard this story?

Looked at that apple. Really looked at it, no one had before, not really. Wondered what it meant. Wondered if he could describe what had happened mathematically. Tried. Did. Learned that when we fall to the earth, the earth also falls, a little, toward us. So that in fact there is no falling, but a moving toward. Tremendous thing. What Newton found: that the world would fly to pieces, but for a great force, a power in every single body in the world, which pulls it ceaselessly toward every other body, which is pulled ceaselessly toward it in turn. No matter what.

We learned what holds the world together, in the plague.

(GRAUNT *turns to look at* SARAH. *Then he crosses to her and holds out his hand. She looks at it. From the beginning of the play until this moment, no one has touched anyone else. She takes his hand and he helps her to stand and walk. The lights fade.*)

END OF PLAY

Printed in the USA
CPSIA information can be obtained
at www.ICGtesting.com
JSHW012049210124
55695JS00026B/406